Cornerstones of Freedom

The Transcontinental Railroad

Peter Anderson

CHILDREN'S PRESS®
A Division of Grolier Publishing
New York • London • Hong Kong • Sydney
Danbury, Connecticut

Library of Congress Cataloging-in-Publication Data

Anderson, Peter, 1956-
    The transcontinental railroad / by Peter Anderson.
        p. cm. — (Cornerstones of freedom)
    Includes index, timeline.
    Summary: The history of the Central Pacific and Union Pacific
railroad companies' efforts to span the continent.
    ISBN 0-516-06635-8
    1. Pacific railroads—Juvenile literature.   [1. Pacific railroads.
2. Railroads—History.] I. Title. II. Series.
TF25.P23A53   1996
385' .0979—dc20
[B]   95-33593
                                                  CIP
                                                   AC

"Crazy Judah" wasn't really crazy. He just had some strange ideas. At least they sounded strange to those who doubted his vision of a railroad that would cross America. There had been others who had talked of the need for such a railroad. But did they really believe it could be built through the high peaks of California's Sierra Nevada mountains? Crazy Judah did.

Theodore Dehone Judah

The real name of Crazy Judah was Theodore Dehone Judah, and he sure knew how to build a railroad. By the time he was twenty-eight years old, he had already supervised the construction of several railways in upstate New York. In 1854, Colonel C. L. Wilson came East looking for an experienced engineer to help him build California's first railroad. He offered Theodore Judah the job.

Always eager for a new challenge, Judah happily accepted the colonel's offer. Even though this new job would have been enough to occupy most men, the young engineer still found time to pursue the dream of a much bigger project. Judah roamed the mountain passes of the Sierra Nevada Range, seeking a route for a transcontinental railroad. During the next eight years, members of Congress debated whether or not a transcontinental railroad was a good idea.

Abraham Lincoln, who was elected president of the United States in 1860, felt that such a railroad was indeed a good idea. Lincoln

Abraham Lincoln

believed that west-coast pioneers, whether they were homesteaders in Oregon or gold miners in California, were too isolated from the rest of the country to trade effectively. Tension over slavery had also driven a wedge between the North and the South. President Lincoln hoped that a transcontinental railroad would help bind the country back together.

By July 1, 1862, when President Lincoln signed the Railroad Act, Theodore

Judah's cross-country railroad no longer seemed quite so far-fetched. The Railroad Act allowed for two railroad companies. One would build west from the Missouri River in Omaha, Nebraska. The other would build east from Sacramento, California. The United States government would loan each company the funds and lands needed to build the tracks.

This map shows the routes followed by each railroad.

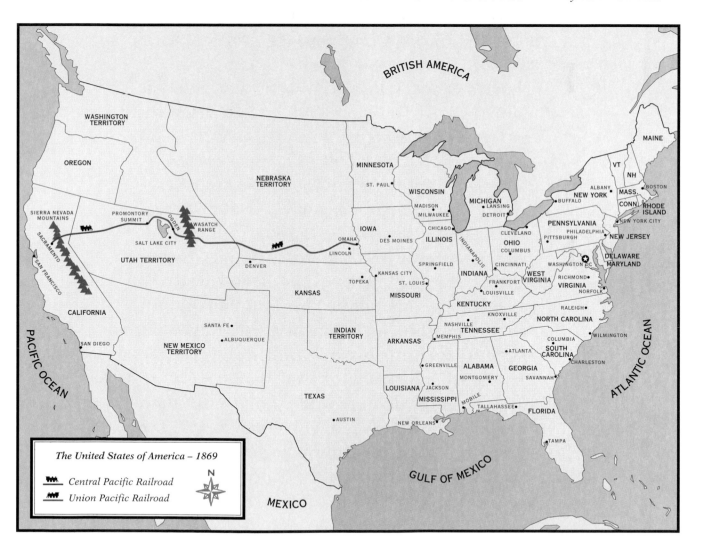

The United States of America – 1869

Central Pacific Railroad

Union Pacific Railroad

N

The Big Four (from left to right): Leland Stanford, Collis P. Huntington, Mark Hopkins, and Charles Crocker

The well-to-do founders of the Central Pacific Railroad Company—Leland Stanford, Collis P. Huntington, Mark Hopkins, and Charles Crocker, later known as the "Big Four"—hired Theodore Judah to blaze the trail for their railroad route. On October 26, 1863, the Central Pacific's first rails were spiked into place, but the man once known as Crazy Judah wasn't there to celebrate. After several disagreements with the Big Four, Judah had gone East to see if he could find other investors to take over the shares of the Big Four. On the way to New York, while crossing Panama to reach a northbound ship, he was stricken with a fever. By the time his ship pulled into New York Harbor, Judah was weak and shaky. His wife, Anna, sent for doctors immediately, but there was little they could do. On November 2, 1863, Theodore Judah died in his hotel room.

Out in the foothills of the Sierras, tracklayers were working overtime that day. Winter was fast approaching. As if winter wasn't challenge

enough, the Central Pacific Railroad Company also had a labor shortage.

Charles Crocker, a big bear of a man at 260 pounds (118 kg), may not have been the most intelligent member of the Big Four, but he made up for that with his strength and stamina. As a supervisor on the Central Pacific, he got up at four o'clock each morning and rode his handcar up and down the rails all day long. Few laborers escaped his inspections. If he came across shoddy work, he freely voiced his criticism.

Crocker had never been one to stand on the sidelines. He wasn't about to let a shortage of laborers limit the railroad's progress. So he thought of a solution. Chinese immigrants, fleeing the upheaval of a revolution in their own country, were pouring into California. Why not hire them?

"I will not boss Chinese!" roared James Strobridge, the construction boss. The Chinese, he insisted, were just too frail to handle heavy railroad labor.

Hadn't the Chinese built the Great Wall of China, asked Crocker? And wasn't that one of the world's largest structures? Strobridge finally agreed to hire fifty Chinese workers on a trial basis.

By December 1865, almost 80 percent of the Central Pacific's workers were Chinese. Big Four partner Leland Stanford, who had once been

Chinese railroad workers

opposed to Asian immigration now spoke out in favor of it. If Chinese laborers had been good for the Central Pacific Railroad Company, he reasoned, they would be good for all of California.

Out on the Great Plains, the Union Pacific Railroad Company had experienced similar delays. Like their west-coast rivals, Union Pacific Railroad organizers had been unable to find the workers and the materials they needed. The armies of the Civil War had already claimed them.

But the war would end in 1865. By the spring of 1866, swarms of men, many of them ex-soldiers, were bound for the West, where they hoped to find work and begin new lives. It was up to Jack and Dan Casement to organize some of these westbound drifters into disciplined work crews.

Jack Casement

Jack Casement was 5 feet 4 inches (1.6 meters) tall; his brother was even shorter. As one railroad worker put it, "they were the biggest little men you ever saw." Jack Casement carried a bullwhip, a .44 caliber pistol, and rarely took "no" for an answer. Of the thousands of men heading west along the Missouri River, he hired only the strongest. It was an odd mix of men. Along with the Irishmen and ex-Union soldiers who made up most of the Union Pacific crew, there were mule skinners, Mexicans, ex-Confederates, ex-convicts, and ex-slaves. Yet as diverse and inexperienced as this group may have been, the Casement brothers saw to it that they worked like an army.

As the Union Pacific "army" pushed out onto the wide-open plains of Nebraska, an advance guard consisted of the surveyors whose job it was to lay out the route. Next came the graders who flattened the road with horse-drawn blades and built the trestles and bridges. Then the bulk of the workers arrived to place the ties, lay the track, and spike down the rails. Behind them chugged a locomotive hauling a long line of boxcars that contained built-in bunks and a dining hall. Farther back were the flatcars that carried all the lumber, rails, and hardware needed for the job.

One of the first steps in building the railroad was to use horse-drawn blades to level the ground.

After the ground was level, workers placed ties—pieces that held the tracks together.

Despite a hot summer sun that scorched the Nebraska prairie, the Union Pacific's army marched on to a steady beat: first, the thump of the rail as it hit the ties; then the ringing of the spike driver's sledgehammer; and the grunting exhale that followed each stroke. To pass the time, tracklayers sang songs that fit the rhythm of their work. The Casement brothers kept up the beat by offering their workers incentives: a pound of tobacco if they could lay one mile (1.6 km) of track between sunup and sundown, three dollars instead of the usual two for a mile and a half (2.4 km), and four dollars for a two-mile (3.2 km) day.

While the Union Pacific crews were making a mile a day out on the Nebraska prairie in the fall of 1866, Central Pacific laborers were chipping away at the solid rock walls of the Sierra Nevada. As far as the Big Four were concerned, losing ground to the Union Pacific meant losing money. Not only did the railroad companies stand to gain government rewards for each mile of track they laid, they were also competing for the prizes of traffic and trade. Whoever got to Utah first would win the trade of cities like Ogden and Salt Lake, the only major settlements in the Great Basin area at that time. Company owners believed that whoever won the race would win the loyalties of the American public. They also believed the winner would receive increased business.

Workers who hauled the rails, laid the tracks, and drove the spikes were more concerned with the immediate challenges they faced each day. In the high country of California, life became increasingly hazardous for Central Pacific Railroad work crews.

Often the only way to make a path around a steep mountain wall was to blast it out. Suspended by rope in a flimsy woven basket, a worker would hand drill a hole in a sheer rock wall. After he inserted the dynamite, he lit the fuse and tugged on the rope to signal to the men above him that the job was done. If all

went well, he could scramble up the cliff fast enough to escape the explosion, while his co-workers above took up the slack. If he wasn't quick enough or if he got hit by the pieces of flying rock that followed a blast, he would end up buried underneath the piles of rocky debris that fell to the valley floor below.

When the advance guard of the Central Pacific chose to tunnel through the mountains, workers spent months in the dim lantern light of dust-filled caverns, chipping away at the heart of the Sierras. Charlie Crocker set up alternating shifts that worked around the clock, seven days a week—drilling, blasting, scraping, shoveling, and hauling rocks out of either end of the Summit Tunnel. But the rock walls were so hard that workers measured their daily progress by the inch.

And then the snow came. Then more came, until the tunnels and the shacks built beside them to house the workers were buried under deep drifts. For an entire winter, the laborers

In the Sierras, Central Pacific crews had to chip away at mountains of solid rock.

who worked on the Summit Tunnel rarely saw the sky. They burrowed through the snow to get from the camp to the tunnel worksite. Vertical shafts cut out of the deep drifts provided the only fresh air and sunlight. With the spring thaw life became easier, but sometimes workers were buried by avalanches until the snow was almost completely melted.

Workers in the Sierras spent most of the winter digging the tracks out from under the snow.

Camp buildings and tents were not strong enough to withstand the blizzards and dust storms of the Plains.

Out on the Great Plains, Union Pacific Railroad workers had other hazards to contend with. Fierce blizzards swept across the prairie each winter. Work continued only when the weather permitted, so Union Pacific crews had plenty of spare time. The ramshackle saloons and gambling halls that sprang up around each camp offered idle workers a chance to spend their paychecks.

Sometimes the tents and shanties that sprang up around railroad camps grew into permanent towns like North Platte, Nebraska; Julesburg, Colorado; and Cheyenne, Wyoming. In other cases, they disappeared soon after the railroad crews moved on. Either way, they earned their reputations as unruly communities full of gamblers and outlaws.

"Law is unknown here," said one observer of North Platte. The inhabitants, he reported, "were having a good time gambling, drinking, and shooting each other."

Cheyenne, Wyoming, in 1868 (left)

Gambling and drinking were among the only activities available to restless railroad workers (below).

If a Union Pacific worker could survive the lawlessness that followed the railroad west, he faced yet another danger. Plains Indians such as the Sioux and the Cheyenne resented the invasion of their traditional hunting grounds. If the railroad was built and settlement followed, as the United States government intended, Indian leaders feared that the buffalo herds they depended on would gradually disappear. While some Indian leaders signed treaties with the government, others were determined to defend their homelands.

"We were feeling angry and said among ourselves that we ought to do something," recalled a Cheyenne warrior named Porcupine. "In these big wagons that go on this metal road, there must be things that are valuable— perhaps clothing. If we could throw these wagons off the iron they run on and break them open, we should find out what was in them and could take whatever might be useful to us."

Just before sundown on August 6, 1867, Chief Turkey Leg and his band of Cheyenne warriors attached a log to the rails with telegraph wire. First came a handcar that flew off the track. The Cheyenne attacked and killed four of the five workers who had come out to fix the broken telegraph wire. Even though William Thompson had been scalped—

"I felt as if my whole head had been taken off,"
he later said—he survived to witness the events
that followed.

"While lying down, I could hear Indians
moving around and whispering to each
other and placing obstructions on the track,"
Thompson said. "After...about an hour and a
half, I heard the low rumbling of a train as it
came tearing along."

*Plains Indians
worried that the
railroad would
destroy their
hunting grounds.*

Cheyenne Indians attack a Union Pacific work crew.

When the train hit the damaged tracks, it tumbled off into a ravine and burst into flames. The engineer and his firemen were killed, but the conductor and three other men somehow escaped. In all the commotion, Thompson grabbed his scalp, which a Cheyenne warrior had dropped nearby, crawled off through the tall grass, and ran across 15 miles (24 km) of prairie to the nearest railroad camp. Surgeons tried to sew his scalp back on but they were unsuccessful. Thompson would live the rest of his life with a scar that told of his violent encounter.

Turkey Leg and his Cheyenne ransacked the wreckage. From the train's cargo, they retrieved ribbons, bonnets, boots, hats, and whiskey. They held a grand celebration. But it was only a fleeting victory. Additional United States cavalry troops defeated the American-Indian resistance.

Dr. Thomas Durant, one of the Union Pacific's principal owners, began to boast of reaching the California border before the Central Pacific had gotten through the Sierras. The Big Four were concerned. Crocker and Strobridge devised a strategy to foil their rivals. They took an advance guard of three thousand Chinese workers across the mountains to lay tracks down the eastern slope of the Sierras and into the Nevada desert.

Even though the Summit Tunnel was still under construction, these advance crews would be able to gain some ground in the lowlands. To do that, they carried hundreds of iron rails, each one weighing 600 pounds (272 kg), through the deep snow. They also had to dismantle three locomotives, haul them across the mountains on special sleds, and put them back together again when they reached the other side.

By December 1867, it seemed as though the fortunes of the California railroad company had begun to change. After two years of slow and dangerous labor, tracks had been laid through the entire length of the 1,659-foot-long (505 m) Summit Tunnel. On December 13, Chinese workers spiked the first iron rails across the California state line into Nevada. By the spring of 1868, tracks had been laid across the eastern slope of the Sierra. Now the Central Pacific Railroad line ran unbroken into Nevada.

The names of the Central Pacific's stations in Nevada—Desert, Hot Springs, Mirage, Granite Point—reflected the experiences that railroad workers would face over the next 500 miles (805 km). Special trains hauling huge wooden water tanks followed the men through the heat waves that rippled up from the desert floor. It would be a grueling summer in this barren land where shade was almost as scarce as water. Nevertheless, Central Pacific Railroad crews averaged 1 mile (1.6 km) of new track each day.

Wagon trains full of supplies followed the crews of the Union Pacific and Central Pacific Railroad Companies.

Plains Indians, such as these Shoshone, reluctantly accepted the building of the railroad.

Paiute and Shoshone Indians joined this strange procession across the Nevada desert. In an effort to foster peaceful relations, Central Pacific Railroad bosses offered their American-Indian neighbors free railroad rides. Indians, both male and female, were also hired. For the most part, they worked harmoniously alongside the Chinese workers.

One day, however, several Paiute storytellers told their Chinese co-workers of giant man-eating snakes that lived in the Nevada desert. These tales were so convincing that five hundred Chinese laborers left that very night. They intended to follow the railroad tracks back to the safety of California, but Crocker sent out several horsemen to bring them back. After the frightened workers were assured that the Paiute had only been joking, they agreed to return to their jobs.

By the winter of 1868, the Central Pacific Railroad crews had laid rails from Sacramento, California, to Carlin, Nevada, a distance of about 446 miles (718 km). Union Pacific Railroad crews had spiked almost 1,000 miles (1,609 km) of track and were closing in on the Utah border. But now it was the Union Pacific Railroad's turn to endure a winter in the high country.

As the December snow draped the high peaks of Utah's Wasatch Range, Union Pacific crews began to build into the mountains. Alarmed by the rapid progress of the Central Pacific across Nevada, Dr. Durant ordered his crews to continue full speed ahead. That year, there would be no permanent winter camp. Instead, Union Pacific workers dragged timbers through snow drifts, chopped at frozen ground with picks and shovels, and blasted tunnels through the red cliffs of Echo and Weber Canyons.

In the rush to get over the mountains, tracks were often laid on snow and ice. Trains crashed into ravines and canyons when the tracks underneath them slid off the grade. Injuries and fatalities plagued the Union Pacific crews all winter. But when workers complained, bosses taunted them with the prospect of losing the great race to their Chinese rivals working on the Central Pacific line. Pride and the promise of higher wages—it was little more than a promise since their paychecks were already several

Train crashes often occurred in the mountains when tracks shifted during the spring thaw.

weeks late—kept them going. On the morning of March 8, 1869, Jack Casement's crews came down from the Wasatch foothills and spiked the first rails into Ogden, Utah.

On the ground at least, victory seemed close at hand for the Union Pacific Railroad. But while the spikers of both railroad companies had been laying claim to additional miles, Big Four investor Collis Huntington had been gaining ground with government officials in Washington, D.C. A map of the planned Central Pacific route to Ogden had been approved by the United States Secretary of the Interior. That meant that the Central Pacific Railroad Company would control the railroad route across western Utah to Ogden.

Advertisements for land tempted settlers to move West.

Still, the Union Pacific Railroad Company would gain compensation for any tracks put down west of Ogden. So the great race continued. The Union Pacific's management was determined to gain whatever financial advantages they could from laying more track into western Utah. The Big Four continued to build frantically toward Ogden, intending to lock up their connection with the cities of Utah.

As yet, a meeting place had not been chosen for the two railroad companies and the crews, it seemed, were more determined than ever to outdo one another. Soon the advance armies of both companies were building grades that paralleled each other. They were so close at times that their dynamite blasts sent rocks and boulders flying (sometimes intentionally) into each other's construction sites.

In a ravine near the Promontory Mountains, 250 teams of horses and 500 men had moved enough dirt and rock to make a flat grade from rim to rim. Meanwhile, Union Pacific Railroad crews were constructing a huge trestle to carry their rails from one side of the ravine to the other. It seemed wasteful to devote so much labor to building two railroad routes when only one was needed. President Ulysses Grant finally stepped in to resolve the matter. He told the two companies to join their tracks at Promontory Summit, Utah.

26

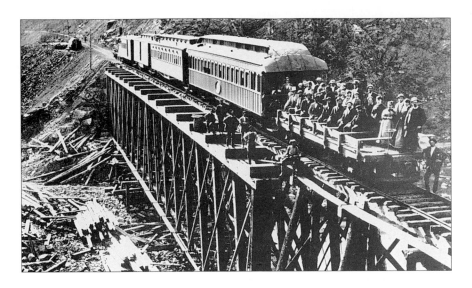

The Union Pacific Railroad crew and the trestle they built at Promontory Summit

Still, one last score remained to be settled. Charlie Crocker had once declared that his men could build 10 miles (16 km) of track in one day. Dr. Durant had seen his Union Pacific crews lay 8 miles (13 km) on one occasion, but 10 miles? He was sure it couldn't be done. Crocker bet him $10,000 that it could. A day or two west of Promontory Summit, he assembled a team of his most devoted tracklayers and set out to prove his point.

At 7:00 A.M., on April 28, with hundreds of men making up the support team that carried water and hardware back and forth along a mile of sagebrush flats, Crocker's tracklayers set out to break the record. Twelve hours later, they had done it: spiked 3,520 rails and 25,800 ties, handled over 1,800,000 pounds (1,260,000 kg) of iron, and built a little more than 10 miles of track.

The spot where Union Pacific crews laid almost one mile of track per hour

*The
Golden
Spike*

For these men, the ceremony that marked
the joining of the tracks was perhaps an
anticlimax. Nevertheless, they gathered at
Promontory Summit on May 10, 1869, to hear
the speeches and see the last spike hammered
into place. They roared with laughter as one
company owner, and then another, took a
swing at the final spike—and missed. A
worker from the audience finally drove the
last spike home.

Then the two locomotives—one from the east
and one from the west—slowly approached
each other. Bottles of champagne were broken
on the final tie to celebrate. Men riding on the
front of each engine clasped hands.

"I see over my continent the...railroad surmounting every barrier," poet Walt Whitman later wrote. "...I hear the locomotives rushing and roaring, and the shrill steamwhistle, I hear the Echoes reverberate through the grandest scenery in the world....Tying the Eastern to the Western Sea."

This monument at Promontory Summit, Utah, marks the completion of the Transcontinental Railroad.

GLOSSARY

avalanche – a large mass of snow, rocks, and ice moving swiftly down a mountainside

boxcar – an enclosed railroad car

Jack Casement used a bullwhip

bullwhip – a long, twisted rod attached to a handle; used for whipping

fireman – a person who tends the fires that drive a steam locomotive's engine

flatcar – a railroad car without walls

Golden Spike – the spike that was used to secure the final rail laid at Promontory Summit; linked the two railroads

grade – the sloping surface on which a highway or a railroad is built

Great Basin – a desert plateau between the Sierra Nevada and Wasatch mountains, covering eastern California, western Utah, and most of Nevada

handcar – a self-propelled cart used by railroad workers to survey tracks and make repairs

mule skinner – a person who drives a team of mules

ramshackle – broken down, not sturdy

sagebrush – a strong-smelling, gray-green shrub, regularly found on the plains of the arid west

trestle

spike driver – a worker who uses a sledgehammer to pound spikes that attach iron rails to the railroad ties

trestle – a framework of vertical or slanting uprights and horizontal crosspieces that provides support for a bridge

TIMELINE

Theodore Judah begins exploring Sierra Nevada mountains

January 8: Central Pacific breaks ground in California

December 2: Union Pacific breaks ground in Nebraska

Central Pacific crew works in Nevada desert; Union Pacific crew crosses Wasatch Range

May 10: Final rail spiked at Promontory Summit

1850 U.S. House of Representatives begins discussing the transcontinental railroad

1853 Army engineers survey four possible routes

1860

1861 Central Pacific Railroad Company is established; Civil War begins

1862 President Lincoln signs Railroad Act

1863

1865 Civil War ends

1867

1868

1869

Central Pacific crew blasts through Sierra Nevada; Union Pacific crew works on Plains

INDEX (*Boldface* page numbers indicate illustrations.)

PHOTO CREDITS

Cover, The Bettmann Archive; 1, ©Tom Till; 2, The Bettmann Archive; 3, Golden Spike National
Historic Site; 4, Library of Congress; 6, (all portraits), Crocker Art Museum, Sacramento, CA: E.B.
Crocker Collection; 7, Denver Public Library, Western History Department; 8, Golden Spike National
Historic Site; 9, Union Pacific Museum Collection; 10, The Bettmann Archive; 11, 13, 14, ©Utah State
Historical Society. All rights reserved. Used by permission; 15, North Wind Picture Archives—hand-
colored print, ©1995 North Wind; 16, Stock Montage, Inc.; 17 (top), ©Utah State Historical Society.
All rights reserved. Used by permission; 17 (bottom), Golden Spike National Historic Site; 19, Stock
Montage, Inc.; 20, North Wind Picture Archives—hand-colored woodcut, ©1995 North Wind; 22, The
Bettmann Archive; 23, Golden Spike National Historic Site; 25, The Bettmann Archive; 26, Stock
Montage, Inc.; 27 (bottom), Southern Pacific Lines; 27 (top), 28 (bottom), ©Utah State Historical
Society. All rights reserved. Used by permission; 28 (top), Golden Spike National Historic Site; 29,
Stock Montage, Inc.; 30 (top), Union Pacific Museum Collection; 30 (bottom), 31 (right), ©Utah State
Historical Society. All rights reserved. Used by permission; 31 (left), Golden Spike National Historic Site

STAFF

Project Editor: Sarah DeCapua
Design & Electronic Composition: TJS Design
Photo Editor: Jan Izzo
Cornerstones of Freedom Logo: David Cunningham

ABOUT THE AUTHOR

Peter Anderson has worked as a river guide, carpenter, writing teacher, editor, and wilderness ranger.
He has written twelve books for young readers on topics related to nature, American Indians, and the
history of the American West.